23 Anti-Procrastination

Habits

How to Stop being Lazy and Get results In your Life

By S.J. Scott

http://www.HabitBooks.com

January 2014
Copyright © 2014 S.J. Scott

Published by Archangel Ink

ISBN 1495472736
ISBN-13: 978-1495472732

Disclaimer

No part of this publication may be reproduced or transmitted in any form or by any means, mechanical or electronic, including photocopying or recording, or by any information storage and retrieval system, or transmitted by email without permission in writing from the publisher.

While all attempts have been made to verify the information provided in this publication, neither the author nor the publisher assumes any responsibility for errors, omissions, or contrary interpretations of the subject matter herein.

This book is for entertainment purposes only. The views expressed are those of the author alone, and should not be taken as expert instruction or commands. The reader is responsible for his or her own actions.

Adherence to all applicable laws and regulations, including international, federal, state, and local governing professional licensing, business practices, advertising, and all other aspects of doing business in the US, Canada, or any other jurisdiction is the sole responsibility of the purchaser or reader.

Neither the author nor the publisher assumes any responsibility or liability whatsoever on the behalf of the purchaser or reader of these materials.

Any perceived slight of any individual or organization is purely unintentional.

4

Table of Contents

Are You a Procrastinator?

It happens to the best of us: There's a looming project that's really important. You *should* focus on completing it. Yet, you come up with a variety of excuses for why it can't be started—Bob needs to be called beforehand, you don't have the right paperwork or you're not sure where to start. Regardless of the "why," we all encounter those times when we procrastinate.

Moreover, there is a cumulative effect to procrastination. Even when you *finally* complete a task, five more have popped up to take its place. No matter how hard you try, it seems like there is a never-ending cycle of things to do.

The truth is we've all procrastinated at some point in our lives. For most of us, it happens every so often—but for some people, procrastination has impeded their ability to live a happy and successful life. This book is written for the latter—anyone who is struggling to get projects and personal tasks completed on a timely basis.

It's not that hard to stop procrastinating. Really, all you have to do is form the *same habits* used by countless successful people and make them part of your routine. While these people often have the same fears and limitations as you, they're able to take consistent action because they've <u>trained</u> themselves to do so.

In this book *23 Anti-Procrastination Habits*, you will discover a catalog of ideas to help you overcome procrastination on a daily basis. Whereas many books provide a simple list of tips, you'll learn *why* a specific strategy works, *what* limiting belief it eliminates and *how* it can be immediately applied to your life. In short, you will learn the root causes of your procrastination and how to overcome them.

Who Am I?

My name is S.J. Scott. I run the blog Develop Good Habits (http://www.developgoodhabits.com)

The goal of my site is to show how *continuous* habit development can lead to a better life. Instead of lecturing you, I provide simple strategies that can be easily added to any busy life. It's been my experience that the best way to make a lasting change is to develop one quality habit at a time.

For most of my life, I struggled with procrastination. In high school and college, I was that guy who crammed the night before a big test. My papers were chronically late. And I couldn't remember to follow through on the simplest of promises.

It was 2003 when I finally did something about this problem. When I first started my online business, I discovered a simple truth: "You are 100% responsible for your life." This one statement made me realize that if I wanted to get results with my business, I had to first change who I was on the inside. Over a course of a few years, I read and implemented information from a variety of books/websites on personal productivity: *Getting Things Done, 43 Folders, Zen Habits, Eat the Frog, The Success Principles, The War of Art* and *The 7 Habits of Highly Effective People*. Plus, I tested a variety of different tactics in the hopes that they would help me overcome procrastination and take action on a consistent basis.

The result?

I currently run a successful Internet business, which includes 37 published Kindle books. Although I haven't fully mastered "personal productivity," I feel like I've come a long way in the past few years. All of this is due to **creating habits** that focus on getting results. In other words, I formed a number of *anti*-procrastination habits.

About 23 Anti-Procrastination Habits

Now, this book isn't about me. I wrote it to help you overcome your problems with procrastination. It includes everything I've learned in the last few years about what it's like to take consistent action every single day. While this book won't *stop* your urge to procrastinate, you'll understand why it happens and how to develop specific habits to overcome this feeling.

The information inside is built on a specific framework. First, we'll go over the psychology behind procrastination. Next, we'll go over the seven excuses that people give when they procrastinate. Third, we'll talk about the 23 habits to overcome these mental obstacles. And finally, I'll help you turn this information into action.

It works in an easy-to-follow manner. You don't have to be crippled by procrastination. In ***23 Anti-Procrastination Habits***, you'll discover a step-by-step blueprint you can use to get results in your life.

Let's get to it.

The Procrastination Habit (or "How to NOT Get Things Done")

You can trace every success (or failure) in your life back to a habit. What you do on a daily basis largely determines what you'll achieve in life.

Habits create routine, and let's face it—most of us run our lives by some sort of routine. We get up in the morning and follow a preset pattern: Take a shower, brush our teeth, get dressed, make breakfast, drive to work, do work and then go home.

Some of us choose to follow *self-improvement* habits: Set goals, read inspirational books, work on important projects and ignore wasteful distractions. Others choose *self-destructive* habits: Do the bare minimum, dull creativity through low-quality entertainment, eat junk food and blame others for their failures in life.

The truth is, habits can be both good *and* bad. They define who we are, what we do and what we can accomplish in life. What's interesting is that every habit is formed by following the <u>same blueprint</u>. Once you learn *how* it works, you can confidently adapt any new routine and follow it on a consistent basis.

Let's say you wanted to write for 30 minutes every day. You would create this habit by following the same blueprint that others have used in the past:

1. Block out a set amount of time each day for this habit.
2. Create a reminder to follow this habit at a specific time.
3. Get started by setting a small goal (like writing for five minutes).
4. Track this habit to make sure you're doing it every day.
5. Have a plan for those days when you're "not in the mood" to write.
6. Scale up your efforts until you're consistently writing 30 minutes every day.

What does this example have to do with procrastination?

Everything.

Both your good and bad habits were formed through repetition. At some point in your life, you developed the habit of procrastination because it gave you the short-term, "feel good" reward of living in the moment. What you probably *didn't* do was to learn how to experience those "lazy feelings" and take action despite them.

One of the biggest reasons why people procrastinate is because a task conflicts with their established habits. Whenever you try to do something that's not part of your daily routine, it takes effort and willpower to complete it. This is especially true if the task is unpleasant.

The simplest solution to eliminating procrastination isn't to fight it. Instead, you need to replace it with good routines that benefit your life.

You'll find that when a difficult task becomes a habit, it becomes hard to put off. Eventually you'll do it without thinking—like brushing your teeth, watching TV and driving a car. All you need is a blueprint that helps you break down any task into a day-to-day process that gets completed.

We all feel tempted to procrastinate from time to time—it's a perfectly normal response when faced with a difficult challenge. The trick to taking action is to understand *why* you're putting it off. In the next section, we'll go over seven major excuses that people give when they feel that temptation to procrastinate.

7 Excuses You Might Have for Procrastinating

It's pretty easy to make an excuse for not starting a task. The trick is to know when a reason is valid and when it's a creative way to avoid taking action. Most of our procrastination feelings come from a subconscious fear or self-limiting belief. When you take time to explore these thoughts, you'll find that it's easy to overcome them and create an action-oriented mindset.

Your mind is an amazing machine. It gives you the power to create anything from your imagination. However, it can also limit your ability to get things done. We often get stuck with a project—not from a lack of desire, but because of maladaptive thought patterns that bounce around in our heads.

The root cause of the "procrastination habit" comes from our self-limiting beliefs. When these thoughts go unchecked, they cause you to make "excuses" for why a project/task can't be completed. However, when you <u>challenge</u> these excuses, you'll see that most of them are caused by hidden fears or destructive habit patterns.

There are seven excuses that people commonly give. Understand why they occur and you'll be one step closer to overcoming procrastination:

Excuse 1: "It doesn't matter."

People often avoid tasks that don't seem important. Sometimes it's not time-critical. Other times it's an unpleasant task that doesn't relate to a long-term goal. And often it requires you to overcome a major fear. No matter what thought runs through your head, there are times when we put off a task because it doesn't seem to be important.

One of the simplest remedies to the "doesn't matter" excuse is to develop the habit of making simple decisions. Either you get busy with completing a task or you have the courage to get rid of it. As you'll learn, one of the best ways to overcome procrastination is to make hard decisions in your life—even if that means eliminating things that once seemed important.

Excuse 2: "I need to do _____ first."

Projects often get hung up because a specific task needs to be completed before doing anything else. Whether it's a phone call, conflicting project, or a simple purchase, it's easy to procrastinate when there's something that needs to be done before anything else.

You can forever eliminate this excuse by developing the habit of completely defining each project. The key here is to break them down into a series of tiny actions that you take on a daily basis. (Credit to *Getting Things Done* for this major insight.)

Excuse 3: "I need more information to get started."

Sometimes this is a valid excuse. We often have tasks that require extensive research before getting started. However, I don't think that it's a valid excuse if you're doing it on a weekly basis.

At the risk of sounding snarky, the simplest solution to this excuse is to *get more information*. Not knowing how to do something should never be a reason to avoid a project. Nowadays, it's possible to learn *any* skill or find someone else to do it for you.

Excuse 4: "I feel overwhelmed and have too much to do."

We all experience those moments when we feel overwhelmed. It seems like no matter how hard we work, our to-do lists never get to-done. Usually this problem happens to people who possess the "Superman mentality" where they feel personally responsible to do everything on their own.

Feelings of being overwhelmed can be eliminated by focusing on important projects and delegating/eliminating the rest. Once you know how to identify what's important, you'll find it's easy to "single-handle" each task and get things done in a consistent manner.

Excuse 5: "I don't have time *right now.*"

Again, this is a completely valid excuse. Sometimes you're focused on a project and it doesn't make sense to start another one. However, the "no time" excuse often turns into a nasty procrastination habit where you're forever putting off important things.

Saying you don't have enough time *now* promises a perfect future when work will be easier, less complicated and fun to do. Subconsciously though, many people make this excuse with the secret hope that the need to do the task will eventually disappear. If you keep delaying action until that mythical "someday," chances are quite high that you'll never tackle this project.

Excuse 6: "I keep forgetting to do it."

People often procrastinate on a task because they *forget* to do it. Sure, we all have those moments when something slips our mind. However, being chronically forgetful is a sign of a deep-seated resistance towards a specific task.

Perhaps you don't think it's important. Maybe you're scared of failure. Or perhaps you're not using an effective organizational system. The point here is that "forgetting" isn't a valid reason for procrastination. At some point, you'll need to make the commitment to either start a task or get rid of it.

Excuse 7: "I don't feel like doing it."

Sure, there will always be unpleasant tasks that we dread. The secret is to know when something *needs* to be done and when it can be permanently eliminated. We often confuse the two by avoiding tasks that might have a positive long-term impact on our lives. That means that even if you don't want to do something, that shouldn't be the only reason for why you're putting it off. The better solution is to analyze *why* you're dreading the task to see if it's a symptom of a larger problem.

Why Most Excuses Are B.S.

Nobody is immune to making excuses. No matter how successful you are, at some point you'll come up with a reason to not take action on a project. That's why it's important to form habits that specifically prevent and overcome the excuse-giving mindset.

For the rest of this book, we'll go over a catalog of positive routines that can be added to your busy day. I've labeled them as *anti*-procrastination habits (APH) because they help you take action even when you're feeling lazy or unmotivated.

Not only will we cover each habit, we'll also talk about how it specifically solves one of the seven common excuses people give for procrastinating on a project. And once you understand *how* to get past this limiting belief, you'll find it's easy to resist the temptation to slack off.

So let's get started with what I consider to be the *most important* anti-procrastination habit of them all.

APH #1: Use the 80/20 Rule to Make Decisions

Excuse Eliminated: "I don't have time *right now.*"

We often procrastinate because it feels like there's too much to do. In my opinion, this weak excuse is a symptom of an inability to define what's truly important in your work and personal life. Fortunately, you can overcome this by ruthlessly applying the 80/20 rule.

This principle, originally stated by Vilfredo Pareto, says you get 80% of your results from 20% of your efforts. Thus, most of your results come from a handful of tasks. You can apply this to procrastination by *only* focusing on the actions that generate a significant result and proactively ignoring the rest.

You can use the 80/20 rule to fight procrastination using this five-step process:

Step #1: Identify the 80/20 tasks

It's important to identify the handful of actions that have the biggest impact on your work. Basically these are the primary reasons you're getting a paycheck. The simplest application of the 80/20 rule is to identify what's truly important and spend more time on these activities. In other words, you should find the tasks that generate 80% of your results and happiness.

What if you can't identify the 80% tasks? Take out a sheet of paper and write down what you do on a daily basis. Next, circle the tasks that produce the best results for your job. Finally, if you have a boss, ask him or her about what is most important.

Do this for your personal life as well. Determine what is *truly* meaningful and what you do simply because it's a habit. Time with family, exercising, volunteering and relationships with others can all be considered 80% because these are the activities that add meaning to your life. Spending hours on Facebook, surfing the Internet and plopping in front of a TV aren't 80% activities because they take up lots of time and provide little reward in return.

It's important to identify your 80% results. Determine what actions *really* generate an income and what *really* brings meaning to your life. This information will help you with making the hard decisions in the next step.

Step #2: Ask a simple question

Your time is a finite resource. Every minute spent on a task is one less minute of your life. So why should you spend time doing something that's not important?

Whenever you're faced with a new potential project or task, ask a simple question:

"Does this task help or hurt my 80% activities?"

Usually we agree to do things from a fear of looking bad or disappointing somebody. However, there's nothing wrong with having an understanding of what's important in your life. If you feel something takes away time from your 80% activities, then avoid doing it at <u>all</u> costs. Remember: Never let other people's priorities become your own.

Now, saying "no" isn't always easy to do if you have a boss. One solution is to approach him or her and explain that you've identified the core activities where you provide the most value. Say that your time will be most effective by focusing on these tasks. Explain that the more time spent on these activities will mean an increase in productivity and job performance. You'll find that most bosses are pretty reasonable when you show how you can do a better job and help *them* get better results.

Step #3: Eliminate or delegate

If you have trouble finding time for a new project, then you'll need to take a look at everything you do on a regular basis. Odds are, you do certain things that take away from your 80% tasks. These are the things that should be eliminated or delegated.

Your project list shouldn't be filled with items that don't matter. If an activity isn't bringing satisfaction or a measurable result, then you should get rid of it. Either pass it along to someone else (delegate) or completely eliminate it.

Again, this might mean having a long conversation with your boss. Simply explain that you need to focus on the important activities and then ask that other activities get passed along to someone else.

Step #4: Don't add, *substitute*

When starting a new project, resist the urge to add it to your pile of things to do. This will only create a feeling of being *overwhelmed*, which is a major cause of procrastination. Instead, a simpler solution is to substitute the project for one that's not generating results.

Remember, your time is limited. If you feel like a new project is important enough to work on, then it should take the place of a low-value activity. That's how you stay focused on 80% activities without getting buried under an avalanche of time-consuming tasks.

Step #5: Practice "creative procrastination"

While this book is designed to help you fight procrastination, sometimes it's okay to strategically put off a task. When you know a project isn't an 80% activity, then it's perfectly fine to put it down on a "someday" list. You'll delay this action with the understanding that you'll only do it if it becomes more important later on in your life.

The key to creative procrastination is to make a habit of reviewing this "someday" list. My suggestion is to go through it during a monthly review where you track goals and determine if you have time to start new projects (more on this later). You don't have to take action on these ideas, but you should at least consider them from time to time.

Habit Implementation

Practicing 80/20 is a skill that takes awhile to develop. At first, it'll be difficult to let go of the projects you once thought were important. Eventually, however, you'll develop an intuitive understanding of what is valuable and what is a waste of your time.

To get started, I recommend doing the following:
1. Run a monthly review that goes over your daily activities.
2. Identify the 80% activities that generate the most results.
3. Eliminate or delegate the activities that aren't part of your 80%.
4. Ask, *"Does this task help or hurt my 80/20 activities?"* when a new project pops up.
5. If it's worth pursuing, substitute it for another project. Don't add it to a list of things to do.
6. Practice creative procrastination on the tasks that aren't important.

You'll discover it's easy to fight procrastination by focusing on the activities that provide the biggest return for your time investment. Apply the 80/20 rule and you won't experience that feeling of being overwhelmed. You won't be stressed about having a miles-long to-do list. Instead, you'll take dynamic action on the most important things in life.

APH #2: Relate Every Action to a S.M.A.R.T. Goal

Excuse Eliminated: "It doesn't matter."

It's easy to self-sabotage your day by not creating priorities. The end result is you're often focused on doing low-value activities that don't generate significant results.

Really, the most effective strategy for overcoming procrastination is to improve your ability to <u>choose</u> what projects should be worked on and what projects should be avoided.

We've all made excuses for putting things off, but if you take the time to explore your thoughts, you'll see that most excuses are due to a subconscious feeling that the task isn't that important.

What's the solution?

It's simple: Make a habit out of relating every single task to a goal. Whenever you're about to start something, ask yourself how it fits in with your long-term plans. If it's directly tied to a written goal, then make time to do it. However, if a project doesn't relate to a goal, then don't be afraid to delegate or completely eliminate it.

Setting goals will be your secret weapon in the fight against procrastination. Knowing what's important creates a framework for your daily routine. No longer will you be paralyzed over a specific task. Instead, you'll take action because you'll know how it fits in with your long-term plans.

You can implement this habit by regularly setting S.M.A.R.T. goals, which is an acronym for: **S**pecific, **M**easurable, **A**ttainable, **R**elevant and **T**ime-bound.

Here's how it works:

S: Specific.

These are your six "W" questions: *Who, what, where, when, which and why.* Answering these questions provides a quick way to create a clear goal with a measurable outcome:

- Who: Who is involved?
- What: What do you want to accomplish?
- Where: Where will you complete the goal?
- When: When do you want to do it?
- Which: Which requirements and constraints might get in your way?

- Why: Why are you doing it?

Here's a great example of a specific goal:
"On May 16th, I will deliver a powerful 15-minute presentation to my boss, giving an update on the Nexus project."
This example shows a complete lack of ambiguity. At the end of the 16th of May, you'll know whether it was achieved or not.

M: Measurable

The second aspect of S.M.A.R.T goal setting is to create an outcome that can be measured. At some point, you want to know—without a doubt—that you've reached this goal.

As an example, *"Give a speech"* isn't a measurable outcome. On the other hand, *"Deliver a 15-minute speech"* is something you can quantify. Either you do it or you don't.

Get ultra specific with your goals. Don't just say you'll "learn public speaking." Instead, create a series of metrics that focuses on continuous improvement.

A: Attainable

Make sure your goals are achievable. Set ones that are challenging, but can be accomplished with hard work. Using the example above, you shouldn't set a short-term goal of speaking at a national conference if you've never delivered a speech in public before. A better goal is to give a great speech to a small crowd or at a local Toastmaster's event.

Now, that doesn't mean you should avoid going after big goals. Whenever you accomplish something, create a new, more challenging goal. Keep pushing the envelope with what you *think* is possible with your life. Perhaps in a year or so you'll find yourself on stage at that national conference.

R: Relevant

Every goal should be relevant to what *you* want. It shouldn't be pushed on you by parents, a spouse or friends. It should focus on outcomes that you *truly* desire.

You will need to be the one who is interested in taking action. When goals come from a personal passion, it's easier to complete them on a daily basis.

T: Time-bound

Tie your goals to a specific timeframe. Personally, I like to set two goals: one short-term goal for the next month and one long-term goal for the three-month mark. Setting immediate goals helps them stay in the forefront of your mind and makes them more achievable.

A goal isn't, *"I'll give a speech."* Instead, it sounds like this: *"On May 16th, I will deliver a powerful 15-minute presentation to my boss."*

Goal setting isn't just for work. In fact, it should be a part of every decision you make in life. Remember, you're trying to overcome procrastination, so you need to look at each task and see how it fits into your long-term plans. This means you should set goals for each of the following:

- Education (both formal and informal)
- Career or business
- Health and fitness
- Hobbies and recreation
- Relationships
- Religion
- Financial
- Public service

You don't need to focus on all of them at once. Instead, it's better to create goals for areas of your life that have a *current* personal significance.

Finally, you should understand the difference between **two types of goals** and how they can impact your capacity to get things done.

First are the *performance goals*, where you focus on the effort, not the outcome. While you'd like to hit a specific milestone, you don't consider it a failure if you don't hit this mark. For instance, a performance goal would sound like this: "On June 1st, I will have a completed 15,000-word book published on Amazon's Kindle platform."

Next are *outcome goals* where you'd like to achieve a specific, measurable outcome. While the performance is important, your primary concern is to hit that number. If you don't, then the goal is considered to be a failure. As an example, you could adapt the above example to this: "On June 1st, I will have an Amazon

Kindle book that generates an average of 10 sales a day."

For the most part, I recommend creating performance goals instead of outcome goals. What's most important is to develop the habit where you're pushing yourself and taking action on a daily basis. Outcome goals can be discouraging if you don't hit these numbers. Performance goals are often better because the keep you focused on the process of self-improvement instead of an all-or-nothing outcome.

Habit Implementation

Here's how to use S.M.A.R.T. goals to fight procrastination:

1. Think of what you'd like to achieve in the next three months.
2. Write down S.M.A.R.T. goals for different areas of your life.
3. Create an action plan for each goal (more on this later.)
4. Review these goals on a daily basis.
5. Figure out how every new project relates to a goal.
6. Eliminate/delegate anything that doesn't match your current goals.
7. At the end of the three months, evaluate your overall success.
8. Create new goals and make them more challenging.

It's easy to procrastinate when a task doesn't seem important. Unfortunately, this attitude can have a negative impact on your projects. At some point, you have to make a decision: Either you start a task or you don't.

With S.M.A.R.T. goal-setting, you'll create a list of what's currently important in your life. Then, whenever you feel tempted to start something new, you'll have a framework for making an intelligent decision. Either a task is important enough to start or it should be avoided at all costs.

APH #3: Capture Your Ideas

Excuse Eliminated: "I feel overwhelmed and have too much to do."

Have you ever felt overwhelmed by a to-do list? There are times when we've all felt trapped by the amount of "stuff" that needs to be completed. We do our best to get everything done, but often it seems like there aren't enough hours in the day to do it all.

What's interesting is this feeling of "overwhelm" isn't due to the number of uncompleted tasks. It usually comes from how you process ideas and action plans. According to the Zeigarnik Effect (http://www.developgoodhabits.com/zeigarnik-effect/), any incomplete thought will occupy the mind until you either do it or write down a plan for *how* you'll do it. In other words, if you're not regularly emptying the ideas in your head, they will negatively impact your ability to stay focused on present tasks.

The Zeigarnik Effect directly affects procrastination because it often causes us to avoid taking action when we have a hundred things to do every day.

What's the solution?

Create the "idea capture habit" where you never let a thought go unrecorded.

Even the simple act of writing down a thought and filing it away for future reference helps you stay focused on current projects. That's why capturing an idea "completes the loops" that often block our ability to get things done. In other words, when your mind is filled with random thoughts, you're not 100% committed to the task at hand.

The truth is, we're constantly bombarded by ideas. Sometimes they'll pop up at random moments— like while exercising, mowing the lawn, driving or painting a room. Other times you'll even wakeup in the middle of the night with a brilliant idea. No matter when inspiration strikes, you need to put them into a single, central location.

There are *two ways* to capture ideas.

The first is the old-fashioned, pen-and-paper approach. Simply carry a notebook wherever you go and use it to record the thoughts and ideas that pop up. My favorite notebook for recording ideas is the Moleskine Notebook, which can be found on Amazon (http://www.developgoodhabits.com/moleskine-kindle).

The next option is Evernote http://www.evernote.com, which is available on a variety of desktop platforms and mobile apps. This tool allows you to capture information like voice recordings, photographs, personal notes and Web page snippets. What's great about this tool is you can easily organize each piece of information for future, instant retrieval.

You might feel it's corny to write things down, but you'll be amazed at the usefulness of this habit. Do it daily and you'll have a clear mind that allows you to *completely* focus on a current project.

As we've discussed, procrastination comes from a feeling of being overwhelmed. It's hard to concentrate when you're worried about a hundred other things. With the idea capture habit, you'll create a relaxed feeling because every thought will be completed at the appropriate time.

Habit Implementation

Here's how to develop the habit of capturing ideas:

1. Carry a tool for capturing ideas wherever you go.
2. Add every thought, the second it pops into your head.
3. Go through these notes once a week.
4. Make a plan for taking action on every idea.

It's been said that everyone, at some point in their life, gets a million-dollar idea. I'm not sure if this is true or not. What I *do* know is that great ideas are a common experience. What's *uncommon* is becoming one of those people who meticulously records every thought that pops up. Developing this habit (in conjunction with a few others that we'll discuss) can help you become better at taking immediate action in your life.

APH #4: Create a 43 Folders System

Excuse Eliminated: "I keep forgetting to do it."

Tasks have a way of slipping through the cracks when you don't have a good organizational system. While we've already talked about the importance of the idea capture mechanism, it's one thing to record a thought and it's a whole other thing to remember to *take action* on it. The simplest solution for remembering everything is to develop the 43 folders habit.

While David Allen talked at length about using an intelligent filing system, it was Merlin Mann who gave this technique the clever name of *43 Folders*. You can read about an overview of the 43 folders system in this post http://bit.ly/LQiArM.

To summarize, the 43 folders creates a systematic approach for following up on ideas. To start, you organize a filing cabinet with 12 main folders for each month. Next, you'll add 31 folders, which represents the maximum number of days in every month. This gives you a total of 43 folders. The 31 folders are put in numerical order, right behind the current month, and then the remaining 11 months are put behind the days, like in the image below:

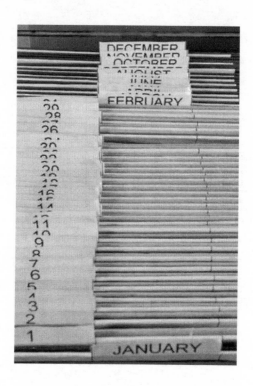

During a weekly review or monthly review (more on this later) you'll put reminders to follow up on certain tasks/projects on a specific date. Then the only thing you'll need to do is create the habit of checking these 43 folders every single day and take action on any task.

Habit Implementation

Developing the 43 folders habit requires a few expenditures, but it's a worthwhile investment to get on the path of never forgetting an important item. Here's how to get started:

1. Dedicate a part of your home for processing paperwork and tasks.
2. Buy a simple filing cabinet and 50 folders with labels.
3. Put every task or idea into a central location.
4. Review these items as part of a weekly review.
5. Schedule a month/day to go over potential projects or tasks.
6. Rinse and repeat, to go through all of this paperwork.
7. Create a daily reminder to go through the current folder for that day.

The 43 folders habit provides a simple mechanism for never forgetting an idea. When you create a reminder to follow up on tasks, your mind won't be occupied with random open loops. Instead, you'll be free to focus on current tasks and projects.

APH #5: Create Project Lists

Excuse Eliminated: "I need to do _____ first."

Procrastination often strikes when a project isn't properly defined. It's easy to put off something when we feel like a specific step must be taken *before* we get started. In truth, this excuse is a way of saying that you haven't properly defined the specific action steps. The solution is to clearly define every task that needs to be done for every single project.

It's scary to begin a new project. We often avoid taking action because something seems too difficult or challenging. When you break down everything into easy-to-complete action steps, you'll find that it's not hard to get things done.

With a project list, you'll break down a huge task into bite-sized chunks. All you have to worry about is doing that *next* step—not the tenth item on your list. You fight procrastination by systematically completing each item on this checklist. You don't worry about the results of the project, you simply do the work.

Create a project list for every aspect of your life. So, if you have multiple things to do, then you'll need multiple lists. For instance, you could make a list for each of these five projects:

1. Start a new exercise routine.
2. Quarterly presentation at work.
3. That novel you've always want to write.
4. Updating your financial records.
5. Installing a new roof.

Maintain a separate sheet for each project. Start by identifying the goal or what you'd like to achieve and then work backwards by identifying the <u>actionable</u> steps along the way. Keep drilling down. Your goal is to create a list of interconnected steps by asking one simple question: *"What's the next action?"*

The key to this habit is to focus on specific, single-action steps. Avoid nebulous statements like "Figure out how to do ___." Instead, write down the *exact* step you need to get it checked off your list.

EXAMPLE:

Let's say you have a new project to start an exercise routine. Here's how you'd break it down into a simple process:

1. Brainstorm the types of exercise you enjoy (cardiovascular, strength training, martial arts or yoga).
2. Research each one to see which has the best long-term benefit.
3. Pick the one exercise program you'll add to your routine.

4. Research different training options (gym vs. home workout).

5. Talk to three different gyms and get details on what they offer.

6. Pick the program that best fits your lifestyle.

7. Sign up for or purchase the training program.

8. Create a daily habit to follow this new exercise routine.

To be honest, even this list might be too broad. If you're having trouble completing these items, you could break them down into smaller action steps. Here's how that would look for action item #1 (brainstorming the types of exercise you enjoy):

1. Research the benefits of running.
2. Research the benefits of walking.
3. Research the benefits of yoga.
4. Research the benefits of cross-fit.
5. Research the benefits of strength training.
6. Research the benefits of martial arts.

Finally, it's important to update this list as a project evolves. You'll get new information along the way, so it's important to add items to this list. Keep taking action, crossing off tasks and working your way through a project until it's completed.

Habit Implementation

Here's a simple process for developing the project list habit:

1. Buy a three-ring binder or notebook.
2. Dedicate a page for each current project.

3.   Think of the primary goal or outcome for the project

4.   Write down the action steps that need to be completed.

5.   Do *at least* one item on this list every day.

6.   Update this project as you get feedback from your actions.

You might think that this habit is needless busywork, but you'd be surprised at how often procrastination strikes when there's an uncertainty of where to start. The project-based approach works because you're constantly taking action. You're not succumbing to a *fear of failure*. Instead, you're taking action and learning valuable lessons—even when you experience a minor failure.

APH #6: Create Checklists for Everything

Excuse Eliminated: "I need to do _____ first."

Sometimes it's easy to procrastinate on the tasks you've done a hundred times before. Often this happens due to a lack of an established process. A simple fix is to create a system for every multi-step task in your life.

Think of McDonald's as a great example. They make an inferior hamburger, and the quality of their other food is also pretty bad. The reason McDonald's is a fast-food empire is because they follow a *system* for every aspect of their day-to-day operations. They have a process for making French fries, one for cooking hamburgers and another for taking an order. Odds are, they have a system for cleaning the toilet.

McDonald's doesn't leave room for interpretation—they give detailed (but easy to follow) instructions to each employee. All somebody has to do is follow these checklists and they'll do an adequate job.

Even if you detest their food, you can learn a lot by following the example of McDonald's. If you do a certain task on a regular basis, then you should turn it into a step-by-step checklist.

It's easy to systematize a process. Take a few hours one day and analyze what you do on a weekly basis. Find those tasks that require multiple steps (so "check email" wouldn't need a process, but "prepare the TPS Report" would definitely work). Once you've identified all your processes, turn them into step-by-step systems. This is similar to creating a project list (APH #5) where each item requires a <u>single action</u>.

My advice is to do this for all aspects of your life—including personal obligations like finances, household chores, packing for a vacation or planning that next party. By creating a system *one time*, you'll have a blueprint that can be reused every time you need to do that task.

EXAMPLE:

Let's say you're required to give a 15-minute project briefing *every week* at work. Instead of doing it off the top of your head, you'd create a step-by-step checklist of what needs to be completed:

1. Map out an overview of what the briefing will cover.
2. Speak with team members about their current challenges/obstacles.
3. Collect related data, metrics and statistics.
4. Organize the information into a logical order.
5. Create a rough draft of the presentation.

6. Get feedback from team members and ask for their input.
7. Write the 2nd, 3rd and final version of the presentation.
8. Practice it until you're comfortable with the material.
9. Give the presentation.

See how this works? Simply create a process for everything you do and you'll always have a specific action to take when you're starting a routine project.

Habit Implementation

It's not hard to create checklists for every routine, multi-step process. In fact, you can do it by developing a habit that's similar to defining a project:

1. Use the same three-ring binder or notebook as your list of projects.
2. Dedicate a page for each routine process.
3. Write down the action steps that need to be completed.
4. Follow it, step-by-step, whenever you're doing the routine task.
5. Look for ways to improve and update this process.

Creating a process checklist might *seem* like extra work. Some might argue that it could cause you to procrastinate instead of fixing the problem. However, I think the reverse is true. Having a step-by-step checklist for routine tasks makes it brain-dead simple to complete tasks. You get to leave out the guesswork and simply follow each step along the way.

APH #7: Batch Similar Routine Tasks

Excuse Eliminated: "I keep forgetting to do it."

We all have those small tasks that take a few minutes to complete, but often slip through the cracks during a busy day. These are the reverse of projects or processes; they're single-action items that are important and need to be completed on a regular basis. It's easy to forget about them, unless you've developed the specific habit of doing them every day. A simple solution to doing them consistently is to batch these small tasks together.

Batching is similar to the process checklist we just discussed. The difference is that you use specific time/environmental cues to act as reminders to get them done.

For instance, I batch together a series of important tasks during my morning routine. In fact, it works as a step-by-step process where I go from waking up to sitting down in front of my computer, ready to start my writing habit:

1. Wake up sometime between 6:30 and 7:30.
2. Walk into the bathroom.
3. Wash my face and weigh myself.
4. Go back into the bedroom and make the bed.
5. Change out of pajamas into normal clothes.
6. Walk into the kitchen, drink one pint of ice cold water with lemon.
7. Grab/make a breakfast shake, a small piece of fruit and two vitamins.
8. Walk into my office, fire up the computer.
9. While the computer is booting, review my goals and eat breakfast.
10. 10 Take my vitamins.
11. Update my habit tracking from the previous night.
12. Start my day by writing for one to two hours.

I'll admit that it's a bit OCD to turn a routine activity into a checklist, but I found it's easy to remember to complete small tasks when they're batched together into a process. Moreover, following this routine creates a number of "small wins," so by the time I start writing, I feel energized and ready to produce great content.

Another application of this habit is to combine a time-blocking strategy like the Pomodoro technique (more on this later.) We all have those tasks that are similar, but require a different type of action. Often it makes no sense to devote an entire period of time to them. A simpler solution is to batch them together into a step-by-step process.

As an example, I follow a "communication process" every single day. This is a simple routine where I do the following:

1.   Go through every email account and "single-handle" each message. When I'm done, my inbox is completely empty.
2.   Schedule any tasks and appointments created by an email message.
3.   Respond to any comments on my two blogs.
4.   Go to my social media accounts (Google+, Twitter and Facebook); respond to any direct messages, create small interesting pieces of content and interact with others.
5.   Check Elance to respond to current outsourcing projects.

Using a batching method to handle small activities has a number of positive effects. First, you'll complete those small commitments that need to be done on a daily basis. Next, you'll avoid a potential "time-suck" by managing your time with a ticking clock in the background. Finally, you'll free up more time to work on the projects that produce 80% of your results.

Habit Implementation

Once again, the best way to apply this habit is to adopt a process-minded attitude towards those small, but important, daily tasks. Here's how to do it:

1.   Identify small tasks that are similar in action and outcome.

2.   Group them together into a logical order.

3.   Create a step-by-step process and add it to a three-ring binder.

4.   Schedule a block(s) of time each day to follow this habit.

Handling tasks in batches is a great way to get things done in a rapid-fire manner without being sidetracked. By creating a process, procrastination doesn't become an option. You won't "choose" what to do next—you'll simply follow what's written down on the list.

APH #8: Single-Handle Processes and Projects

Excuse Eliminated: "I feel overwhelmed and have too much to do."

When we get overwhelmed, we often use multitasking to get back on track. The problem? Multitasking often causes more problems than it solves. Usually when you split your attention, you're giving half the effort and producing half the results. Instead of trying to cram separate activities into one block of time, you can develop the habit of "single-handling" activities.

The single-handling habit requires you to focus on closing loops on projects/processes as soon as possible. On a daily basis, this means taking immediate action on every task that comes across your path. For instance, many people have the habit of reading emails on their phone. But, if you follow the principle of single-handling, you'd remove the email application from your phone and only read messages when you're ready to take action on them.

Single-handling is also an effective strategy for long-term projects. It's common practice for people to start multiple things at the same time. The smarter strategy is to focus on completing one project before starting another. Not only will this habit help you get more things done, you'll become far more motivated about the task.

To illustrate this point, let's say you're a graphic artist who relies on residual income from each completed project. Right now, you have five weeks to complete five jobs. Pick the option that you think would be more effective:

- Option A: Work a little bit on each, finishing all five on the fifth week.
- Option B: Complete one project per week.

You're right if you chose "Option B."
Here's why...

On week #1, you complete project #1. Week #2, you complete project #2, while earning money from project #1. On week #3, you complete project #3, while earning income from projects #1 and #2. The same goes for weeks #4 and #5.

Now, most people don't have the benefit of earning residual income. But, you can still gain the benefits of single-handling tasks throughout your life. When you have the habit of completing what you start, you'll close more of the loops that suck away mental energy and create the motivation that's required for producing great work.

Habit Implementation

The single-handling habit takes awhile to develop. To be honest, I still occasionally slip and end up doing multiple projects at the same time. But I always get better results when I delay/eliminate other projects to focus on one.

The best way to implement the "single-handling habit" is to do the following:

1. Start a daily routine *only* when you're committed to completing it.
2. Prioritize projects according to immediacy and their long-term benefit.
3. Work on Project A until it's fully completed.
4. Rinse and repeat with Projects B, C, D and E.
5. Avoid the risk of backsliding by doing a weekly review and analyzing your current project priorities.

You'll find that single-handling tasks/projects can have an amazing impact on your productivity. Furthermore, you're less likely to procrastinate because you'll create motivation for the task and feel excited as the deadline is drawing close.

APH #9: Schedule a Weekly Review

Excuse Eliminated: "I keep forgetting to do it."

We often procrastinate—not out of laziness, but because we simply forget about a specific promise or task. Even if you're good at capturing ideas, it's impossible to take action if you don't follow up on them. Moreover, you'll often struggle to complete specific actions if you're not making plans for *when* they'll be completed. All of this can be solved by developing the habit of the weekly review.

The weekly review is a concept I originally learned from David Allen's *Getting Things Done*. While I recommend *all* of his teachings, I found the weekly review concept to be particularly helpful for preventing procrastination. It's a simple process. Once a week (I prefer Sundays), look at the next seven days and schedule the activities/projects you'd like to accomplish. In addition, process all the notes from your idea capture mechanism and process any new paperwork.

You can accomplish all of this with three simple steps:

Step #1: Ask Three Questions

When starting a weekly review, ask three questions that will shape the focus of what you'll do over the next seven days:

Q1: What are my personal obligations?

Do you have a planned family activity? Are you going on a vacation? Do you have any personal appointments, meetings or phone calls? Is there something fun you'd like to do?

I've found that it's hard to complete projects when I have a lot of personal obligations. So it's better to *plan* for these potential interruptions rather than have them suddenly pop up and derail the next seven days. Honestly, you'd be better off reducing your output instead of trying to be a superhero by filling each day with 16 hours of activities.

Q2: What are my priority projects?

Sometimes a certain project takes precedence over everything else. This is the time when it's okay to *purposefully* procrastinate on other things. I'm a firm believer in focusing on one thing at a time. You can use the weekly review to focus your efforts on completing a single project that will have the biggest impact on your professional or personal life.

Q3: How much time do I have?

This question is extremely important. If you know your time is limited (like having a need to focus on a single project), then you should give yourself permission to not begin anything new.

In a later section, we'll talk about developing the "time blocking" habit. For now, just know that it's important to track the number of *actual* hours that you put into work and personal projects. Once you know, on average, how much time you spend doing different activities, can you use this third question to decide where to best allocate your time and energy.

Step #2: Schedule Project Tasks

After answering these three questions, map out the next seven days. The simplest way to do this is to look at your project lists (APH #5) and schedule time where you can follow-up on the most important activities.

Take a close look at each project. Identify the items on these lists that will have the biggest impact on your professional and personal life. Then, schedule time in the next seven days where you can take action on these tasks.

Step #3: Process Captured Ideas

Okay, so you have a notebook/app filled with great ideas. How do you follow up on them? The simplest solution is to process each one and either do it immediately or schedule a time when you can act on it.

This entire process can easily be squeezed into a weekly review.

Simply open up your idea capture mechanism and go through each note. Basically you'll decide one of two things:

1—The idea is actionable.

I'm a big fan of David Allen's "two-minute rule." The idea here is if an idea takes two minutes to complete, then you should do it immediately. No putting it off and no scheduling time for a follow up. *Just do it.*

Now, if an idea is something you'd like to immediately implement, then write out a step-by-step plan for how you'll do it. (Remember our discussion of the Zeigarnik Effect and how *not* having a plan can impede current projects.) Simply write down a series of actions you'll take on this idea and then schedule these ideas into your week.

2—The idea is not actionable.

Sometimes it's not the right time for a great idea, but you still want to follow up on it. That's when you'll implement the "43 folders habit." Simply pick a date to follow up on the idea and then put a reminder inside the appropriate section. That way, you'll never miss out on a potentially important idea.

Habit Implementation

Obviously, you won't need to do this habit every single day. However, doing it on a weekly basis helps you identify the tasks that are important, which ultimately allows you to overcome procrastination. You can implement this habit by doing the following:

1. Schedule a specific time each week for a review session.
2. Start by asking the three questions to identify important projects and personal obligations.
3. Block out time for each item and plan out your week.
4. Process your notes, take action on two-minute tasks and create reminders to follow up on non-actionable ideas.
5. Keep doing this weekly review, *even* if you don't have anything important coming up.

Overall, the weekly review is important for fighting procrastination. When you make a plan every seven days, you'll create a sense of urgency to focus on the important things. Develop this habit to identify critical upcoming projects and to free your mind from distractions.

APH #10: Do a Monthly Review

Excuse Eliminated: "I feel overwhelmed and have too much to do."

We've already talked about the weekly review, but it's equally important to do a *monthly* review. While the monthly review only requires a few hours of your time, it's another solution to the excuse of being overwhelmed.

In a way, the monthly review is like a report that businesses give to their shareholders. It identifies what's working, what's not and how things can be improved. By doing this once a month, you'll "course-correct" the tasks that don't produce results.

There are a few things you should do during a monthly review:

#1: Review S.M.A.R.T. Goals

Even though you should review goals on a daily basis, it's important to take 30 minutes each month and make critical adjustments. Sometimes you'll find that a long-term goal becomes less important and other times you'll have a new goal to complete. During the monthly review, you'll go through each of these goals to see if they need to be changed, deleted or enhanced.

#2: Identify Potential New Projects

By creating a number of "future follow-ups," you'll invariably create a long list of ideas that require constant review. During the monthly review, go over each of these items to see if it's a project that's worth adding to your project list.

#3: Create Project Lists

Just like you would with a weekly review, you should create a step-by-step list of any idea you'd like to implement. Start with the outcome and then work backwards on what needs to be done. Get everything on paper and then add these tasks to the three-ring binder you started for APH #5.

#4: Ask 80/20 questions

While we've already talked about analyzing tasks through the lens of the 80/20 rule, I recommend you do it at least once a month during a review session. The best way to analyze your tasks is to ask the questions that Tim Ferriss outlines in his book *The 4-Hour Workweek*.

- What 20% of sources are causing 80% of my problems and unhappiness?

- What 20% of sources are resulting in 80% of my desired outcome and happiness?
- What are the top three activities that I use to fill time to feel as though I've been productive?
- Who are the 20% of people who produce 80% of my enjoyment and propel me forward, and which 20% cause 80% of my depression, anger and second-guessing?

Ask these questions once a month and you'll discover what's holding you back from getting things done on a regular basis. Sometimes it's certain people who suck away our emotional energy like a vampire. Others times you'll identify certain habits that cause an unproductive state. And once in awhile you'll discover that projects you once considered important are actually limiting your ability to get results.

Habit Implementation

It's not hard to do a monthly review. All you need is a few hours and willingness to be honest about what's *really* going on in your life. Here's a simple process for implementing this habit:

1. Schedule an uninterrupted block of time for this review (most people prefer a weekend day).
2. Go through and process each piece of paper like you would do with a weekly review.
3. Review your S.M.A.R.T. goals, adding, deleting or changing your desired outcomes.
4. Identify new projects you'd like to pursue for the next few months.

5. Create a detailed list for each project.

6. Ask 80/20 questions about what you're currently doing, eliminating the tasks that don't have a significant impact on your life.

The monthly review helps you take a hard look at what you're currently doing. Not only will you identify wasteful activities, you'll have a chance to take action on projects that might have been initially dismissed. Develop the habit of doing this once a month and you'll become laser-focused on the tasks that truly matter.

APH #11: Say "No" to Low Priority Activities

Excuse Eliminated: "I don't feel like doing it."

I'm always amazed at how often I'll talk to people who do tasks that they hate. While we all have to do unpleasant things in life, often it's easy to fall into the trap of agreeing to projects simply because we don't want to disappoint others.

While we've talked a lot about not letting excuses prevent you from taking action, sometimes there's a valid point behind the excuse you're giving. If you *really* don't want to do something, then perhaps it's time to let it go.

Habit Implementation

The hardest part of learning to say "no" is how to handle the reactions from others when you're basically telling them that their priorities are not your own. Here's a simple four-step process for doing this.

First, you have to identify the *mandatory* tasks. These are the actions that are part of being a normal, well-adjusted adult. If you go around saying "no" to every request, you won't get very far in life. We all have things that *must be done*, so you might as a well accept that you have to do things, no matter how much you don't like them.

My only advice is to relate each task to an important long-term goal. For instance, even if you hate doing the dishes, think about how completing this daily task leads to a harmonious marriage.

Next, you should carefully analyze each request against your current priorities and projects. During a weekly review, identify the important items that need to be completed. When you get a request to work on something, compare it to your desired outcomes. If they don't match, then have the courage to say "no" to the requester.

Third, you should be upfront with people about their requests. If you know there's no chance you'll follow through, then tell them right away. Honesty really *is* the best policy here. Simply tell the person that you have a few priority projects that require your full attention and you can't afford the distraction. Usually, most people will understand this and anyone who doesn't shouldn't be in your life in the first place.

Finally, try to end the conversation on a positive note. If you can't help a person, recommend someone who can. If you know of a helpful resource, send a link to the person. And if you think that you *might* grant the request sometime in the future, then tell the person you'll reply back on a specific date.

Saying no doesn't make you a selfish person. It makes you someone who clearly understands what's important. By having clear goals, you don't allow the demands of others to distract you from completing important projects.

APH #12: Track Your Progress and Successes

Excuse Eliminated: "It doesn't matter."

We often procrastinate due to a lack of motivation. It's hard to be excited when it seems like you're getting nowhere fast. One simple solution is to meticulously track the progress on any process you're trying to improve.

Peter Drucker said it best with this quote: *"What gets measured gets managed."*

To improve <u>anything</u> in life, you need to develop the habit of tracking goals/projects on a daily basis. Then, whenever you feel a lack of motivation, you can look back on your past successes to see how far you've come.

Tracking has a twofold benefit:

First, you'll get motivation to keep at it. Often, the simple process of doing the same thing every day provides enough of a reason to continue. We all like to achieve small accomplishments. By tracking an action, you'll create a "streak habit," where you're afraid to stop because it breaks the chain. (Read this article to learn more about the streak habit: http://www.developgoodhabits.com/streak-occasional-habits/)

Second, you'll learn from previous experiences. It's easy to forget how far you've come as the weeks and months go by. By tracking your success along the way, you can look back and learn lessons from the accomplishments you've achieved in the past.

For instance, let's say you want to improve your average daily word count while writing. By meticulously tracking the conditions around this habit, you'll see patterns on your most prolific days. Ultimately this is how you identify the perfect environment for cranking out a high word count.

Tracking should be applied to every aspect of your life. I recommend doing it for each of the following:

- How many blocks of time you spend doing *actual* work.
- What foods you eat and their total calories.
- The time/distance/conditions of your exercise program.
- Percentage breakdown of the tasks you do at work.
- How many hours you spend on a side business or personal project.
- Financial records including debt, investments and savings.

Really, anything you do in life should be tracked to some extent. Only by creating careful records are you able to learn from each experience and get the motivation to continue a habit on a daily basis.

Habit Implementation

Developing a tracking habit is an ongoing process. You won't wake up one day with a desire to do a task on a consistent basis. Instead, you'll have to turn it into a daily habit. Here's a simple process for getting started:

1. Take a look at each long-term S.M.A.R.T. goal you've set.
2. Identify a way to *quantify* each into a specific daily action (for instance, publishing a book by November 1st would mean writing a certain word count each day).
3. Make the commitment to do this action every day.
4. Monitor the accomplishment of this habit. My favorite tool for this is the Lift.do app, but you can also find a variety of habit-specific apps on your favorite mobile platform.
5. Update *all* of your tracking at least once a day. I prefer the end of the day, before going to sleep, or first thing in the morning. Usually this takes five minutes to complete.
6. Add a reminder to your weekly and monthly review to go over the metrics you're using to achieve your S.M.A.R.T. goals.

Tracking might seem like a lot of busywork. Sure, it requires a small time investment. However, you'll find that it's a motivating habit for sticking to a goal *and* learning from your daily experiences.

APH #13: Start Your Day with MITs

Excuse Eliminated: "I don't have time *right now.*"

While it's easy to pay lip service to the idea of the 80/20 principle, you'll find that it's hard to focus on important tasks every day when you have a schedule full of conflicting activities. The solution? Don't *find time* for these tasks. Instead, start your day by doing them first thing in the morning.

A few years back, Leo Babauta talked about a concept called Most Important Tasks (MITs) bit.ly/1cVoZfz. The idea here is to identify the tasks that have the biggest impact on your life/business and do them first thing in the morning.

The anti-procrastination habit here is to identify the three tasks that absolutely must be completed by the end of the day. Two should relate to a current a project and one should be part of a long-term goal.

Moreover, one of the three MITs should be a habit that you complete on a daily basis.

EXAMPLE:

Last year, I determined that my primary 80% activity was writing. It doesn't matter *what* project I'm working on, I usually have to do this activity every workday. This means I had to develop the habit of starting each day with an hour or two of writing. From there, I spend the rest of my morning doing the other two MITs that are important for that day. By focusing on important activities right away, I create an energized state where I can work on any project in the afternoon.

Habit Implementation

Developing the MIT habit is surprisingly easy to do. It can be done by completing these five steps:

1. End each day by identifying three important tasks for the next day.
2. Prioritize this list, putting the most critical task at the top
3. Wake up and immediately start working on task #1 until it's completed.
4. Continue by fully completing task #2 and task #3.
5. Spend the rest of your day by focusing on lesser but still important tasks.

I highly recommend developing the habit of the morning MITs. Starting each day with a focus on important tasks is the *ultimate* procrastination killer. Instead of "finding time" to do the critical things, you'll immediately complete them before switching to activities that aren't as impactful on your life. (For more on how to create a powerful morning routine, check out my other book *Wake Up Successful*.)

APH #14: Prioritize Using the ABCDE Method

Excuse Eliminated: "I feel overwhelmed and have too much to do."

While I've had a great experience using the MIT system, I know some people find it to be too restrictive. Often, we'll start the day with a dozen things to do and it's limiting to *only* focus on three core activities. If this sounds like you, then you should prioritize each by using the *ABCDE method* (a concept created by Brian Tracy http://www.briantracy.com).

With the 80/20 rule, we talked about the importance of identifying the tasks that are most important in your life and business. And with the MIT system, we talked about focusing on completing three tasks each day. The ABCDE method is different because you create a ranking system for a list of tasks and systematically work through them. It's different than the other techniques because you'll probably have a lengthy list of tasks that need to be completed:

"A" tasks are mandatory to complete every day. These are like MITs because there are serious, negative consequences to *not* doing them.

"B" tasks are important tasks, but are not considered mandatory for that day. They should be completed only after doing every "A" task.

"C" tasks are nice to do, but don't have a specific negative consequence or timeline.

"D" tasks should be delegated to someone else. While they're important, these items don't require your direct input or action.

"E" tasks should be eliminated. This is when the 80/20 rule comes into effect. If you find a task to be pointless during a weekly or monthly review, then eliminate it from your life.

We often procrastinate because we feel overwhelmed. By prioritizing your lists, you'll discover what's truly important on a daily basis. When you keep procrastinating on an item, then it's an indication that it should be eliminated.

Finally, don't forget about the importance of a daily habit. While a certain task might not be considered "urgent," it's *still* critical for your long-term success. Be sure to make sure this task is added to the list of daily actions.

As an example, my *daily writing* habit is never time sensitive. However, I always consider it to be an "A" task because it forms the foundation of everything I've achieved with my online business. I don't rely on "finding time" to write. Instead, I prioritize each day, so I'm *making* time.

Habit Implementation

The ABCDE method is most effective when done on a daily basis. Here's the simplest way to form this habit:

1. Schedule five minutes each night for the prioritization habit. (You can do it right after updating your habit tracking.)
2. Look at your projects and identify what needs to completed for the next day.
3. Write down each task and place a letter next to each task.
4. Reorganize these tasks on a new piece of paper, putting them in an alphabetical ranking.
5. Start each day with the "A" tasks. Move on to the lower priorities *only* when you've completed the important items.
6. Examine these actions during a monthly review to make sure you're not doing things that can be eliminated or delegated.

We all have different priorities. The trick is to develop a system of identifying what's most important on a daily basis. With the ABCDE method, you'll start each day with a clear-cut list of what needs to be completed and the order in which they should be done.

APH #15: Create a Sense of Urgency

Excuse Eliminated: "I don't have time *right now.*"

According to Parkinson's Law, the time it takes to complete a task directly correlates to how much time you give it. If you have a three-week deadline to do something, odds are you'll be finishing up at the end of day #20. The end result is we'll often create the excuse that we can't do something because there's not enough time. But, if you create a sense of urgency with every task, you'll complete projects faster and develop a larger capacity to get more done with the same amount of time.

A great anti-procrastination habit to develop is to live your life like a task is "due" the next day. It doesn't matter if have a week to complete a project—make a habit of getting things done as quickly as humanly possible. In other words, create a sense of urgency with every task.

There are two ways to do this:

First, create self-imposed deadlines.

Remember, a task will often take as much time as you give it. So why not challenge yourself to do it faster? If something normally takes a week to complete, try to do it in five days. Make it a game to continuously push the pace and break your personal records for accomplishing a task.

Follow this rule *even* if others create the deadline. Let's say your boss sets a project deadline for October 1st. Try to get it in by September 15th. Not only does this help improve your overall job performance, it also gives you more time to work on other important tasks.

Next, use time-blocking techniques.

Multi-tasking can be a dangerous habit to follow. While you *might think* you're successfully doing two things at once, what you're *actually* doing is giving half the effort to each task. (Check out this Mashable infographic for more on this: http://on.mash.to/1hgFfaM) If you regularly multi-task, then you're probably producing inferior work. The simplest solution to this problematic habit is to develop the habit of "time-blocking" your work.

The idea behind time-blocking is to break apart your day into small pockets of work where you're 100% focused on a single task *without* any sort of interruption. That means no checking email, Facebook, texting friends or switching between projects. During that block of time you do that task and <u>nothing else</u>.

Habit Implementation

My preferred time-blocking system is the Pomodoro technique (http://pomodorotechnique.com/), which was started by Francesco Cirillo in the mid-1980s. Cirillo found that you can maximize results by completely focusing on a task for a short period of time and then using small breaks for energy renewal.

Here's how it works:

1. Create a list of tasks to be completed, start with your daily MITs.
2. Prioritize tasks in order of importance.
3. Set a timer to 25 minutes.
4. Work on the first task until the timer rings.
5. Record the "Pomodoro" as a completed task.
6. Take a short break of five minutes.
7. Continue working through Pomodoros until you've completed the first MIT.
8. Repeat this process until you've completed the 2nd and 3rd MIT.
9. For every four Pomodoros (or Pomodori?), take a longer break of 15 to 30 minutes.
10. Continue until you've gone through the important tasks for the day.

It takes awhile to acclimate to the Pomodoro Technique, but when you've done it long enough, you'll find it's easy to get into "the zone" the moment you start a timer.

Overall, it's important to create a sense of urgency with everything you do. Your time is a limited resource, so you should develop the habit of getting tasks completed quickly. Do this often enough and you'll find yourself with more time to focus on the fun things in life.

APH #16: Become Publicly Accountable

Excuse Eliminated: "I don't feel like doing it."

It's amazing how much we're affected by the opinions of other people. We all want to be well-liked and admired, so often we'll force ourselves to do something, simply due to a desire to look good. You can use this fact to your advantage by becoming "publically accountable" for every major goal.

Public accountability works because of a phenomenon called The Hawthorne Effect (http://www.developgoodhabits.com/hawthorne-effect/). From a number of psychological studies, it has been proven that people are more likely to complete a task if they feel like their actions are being observed by others. In other words, it's easy to blow off something if you're the only who knows about it, but you won't do it if people expect you to follow through.

This habit is easy to implement, yet people don't do it because they're afraid of "losing face" in the opinions of others. It means being candid with a select group of people about the mistakes or setbacks you make. On the other hand, being held accountable means you also receive positive feedback and reinforcement.

The simplest way to create public accountability is through the Internet. Nowadays, there are countless websites/apps that help people achieve their goals. Simply find one that's related to the habit you're trying to develop and then connect with like-minded people. Another idea is to use an app like Lift.do that combines social media with habit tracking. Just sign up for specific habits and you'll get encouragement (or "props") from other Lift members.

Habit Implementation

It's not hard to become more accountable for your actions. Here are a few ways to share your efforts and get feedback from others:

- Family and friends (find a buddy to support one another).
- Mastermind Groups (bit.ly/1kdxoyS)
- Habit sharing apps (like Lift.do).
- Habit specific forums.
- Go to local events and meet like-minded people.
- Social media sites like Facebook, Twitter and Google+.
- Blog your results (Wordpress.org and Blogger.com are free).

Now more than ever, it's easy to connect with people who share similar desires and goals. Display them for the whole world to see and you'll be surprised at how much encouragement you'll get back.

While you might get nervous at the idea of making a public declaration, you'll discover that it's easy to avoid procrastination when you feel like people depend on you to follow through with a promise.

APH #17: Start Exceedingly Small

Excuse Eliminated: "I feel overwhelmed and have too much to do."

In psychology, there's a term called the hot-cold empathy gap (http://www.developgoodhabits.com/hot-cold-empathy-gap/). Basically this describes how people can set lofty plans from an analytical "cold" state, but they often forget about what it's like to be in a "hot" state where they're bombarded with temptation. It's kind of like making the promise to swear off sweets, but caving in when you pass by a Cinnabon.

In regards to procrastination, the hot-cold empathy gap often prevents us from starting a goal because that task itself might seem *insurmountable*. Often when you have a challenging goal (like writing for an hour a day), it's hard to develop that initial willpower to get started. When this happens, you'll make the excuse that the task is too overwhelming and you'll do it when you have "more time."

On his blog, Leo Babauta talks about a simple solution to this problem. His advice is to start exceedingly small (http://zenhabits.net/habitses/). Instead of worrying about how much you do a habit, you should simply focus on turning it into a daily routine—even if it's a small amount.

EXAMPLE:

Let's say you'd like to write 1,000 words a day. This can be an intimidating word count if you haven't done it on a consistent basis. However, if you *start small*, it's not hard to average 100 daily words for the first week. Next week you'd do 200. Keep ramping up every week by 100 words and in 10 weeks you'll have successfully developed the habit of writing 1,000 words a day.

The "start small" habit also works well with *established* routines. Often, you'll feel a resistance to getting started with task—even when you've done it a million times. The solution? Make a promise where you'll focus on a small goal, and when you reach that point, you have permission to quit. What usually happens then is you'll get started and then realize the task is not that bad.

I do this *all* the time during my wintertime runs. It's hard to feel motivated to run in a frigid, bleak environment. So I'll often get myself out the door with the promise that I'll only go out for a few miles. And usually by mile two, I'm in a rhythm where the weather isn't that big of a deal.

Habit Implementation

You can start small with basically any task. The trick is to develop the mindset where you push yourself to follow through—even when you're not in the mood. Here are a few ways to get started:

1. Make the commitment to do a daily habit every day, no matter how you feel.
2. Create a small, quantifiable outcome for this habit.
3. When starting out, focus on achieving this small goal.
4. Ramp up the length/time/quantity of the task every week.
5. Agree to *still* do the habit even if you aren't feeling well or don't have the time.

Often, it's hard to get motivated for a challenging task. The quick fix is to agree to start small and build willpower as you develop the habit. Simply commit to always following through (no matter what happens) and eventually you'll be more likely to do it on a daily basis.

APH #18: Reward Yourself

Excuse Eliminated: "I don't feel like doing it."

You've probably heard about the "carrot and stick" approach to motivation. In theory, you can reinforce good actions through a reward system and discourage bad actions by punishing your mistakes. Now, it's been proven that punishment is not an effective long-term strategy for motivation. However, you can overcome a lack of desire for a specific task by creating a small reward system.

First off, you should create rewards throughout the day. Odds are you have a few activities that you enjoy on a regular basis—like reading, hopping on Facebook, checking email or talking to a friend. Instead of doing these activities whenever you feel like it, turn them into a reward for completing a specific task.

Next, create larger rewards for accomplishing *major* goals. Look at your S.M.A.R.T. goals and make a promise to reward yourself for achieving each one. The key here is to make sure the reward doesn't counteract what you're trying to accomplish.

For instance, let's say your goal is to weigh 150 pounds by January 1st. A good reward is to plan a weekend vacation with your spouse if you hit this milestone. However, a bad reward is to go on a pig-out session at Sizzler. See the difference here?

Habit Implementation

Have fun with this habit change. It's designed to take the distracting habits that often cause procrastination and use them to help you stay motivated. Here's how to apply this information:

1. Make a list of fun things you enjoy daily (reading, exercising, social media or talking on the phone).
2. Use a time-blocking system like the Pomodoro technique to work for 25 minutes.
3. Resist all temptation to do anything but that task during this time.
4. Reward yourself with a five-minute break to do a small "fun" activity.
5. Set a timer for these five minutes and get back to work once it goes off.
6. Continue doing your tasks throughout the day and reward each small accomplishment.

On the surface, you might feel like a lab rat doing tricks to get a pellet. However, creating a systematic reward system can help you maximize the results you get with every task. Furthermore, it's great for fighting a lack of desire to do a specific task. When you know it's only 25 minutes until you get to do something fun, you'll create a sense of urgency to get things done.

APH #19: Develop Project-Based Skills

Excuse Eliminated: "I need to do _____ first."

Sometimes it's not enough to plan out a project because you have the legitimate excuse of not knowing how to do something. The solution to that problem is to either *delegate* the task or find out how to do it yourself. Usually people opt for the do-it-yourself approach, so in order to complete a task you'll need to form a brand new skill.

Refer back to the list of steps for a project or a process. Look at each item and ask yourself if you're avoiding a specific task because you don't know how to do it. If so, you can either delegate it to a co-worker or hire a freelancer to do it for you. However, if you feel like the task is important for your personal development, then you'll need to focus on improving your skills for that task.

Fortunately for you, <u>every</u> task in the world has been successfully completed by someone else. All you have to do is take a proactive approach and educate yourself on how to do it.

Habit Implementation

It's not hard to get a crash-course on a particular skill. Here's a six-step process for getting started.

Step 1: Identify the specific skill

First, figure out the exact thing you're trying to learn. For instance, your goal shouldn't be to "become a better public speaker," because that's not an actionable outcome. Instead, it's more effective to have a specific goal in mind that shows you've achieved a certain level of competence.

Using the above example, you could create this goal: "Deliver compelling, step-by-step five-minute YouTube presentations." This is actionable because your success is measurable—either you create the five-minute YouTube videos or you don't.

"How" you learn something is a lot like developing a project list. Get out a piece of paper and write down every step you'd need to take. Start with your end goal and work your way backwards. If there's an unanswered question, then create a task to research it along the way.

Step 2: Focus on one skill

Even if you have a laundry list of things to learn, it's always better to focus on one at a time. Maybe you have a list of "someday" items like running a marathon, learning to juggle, become a great public speaker and being a better guitar player. The trick here is to pick the skills that are *immediately* applicable.

Moreover, think about the impact of how one skill will affect your life. Using the above example, you might decide to focus on "public speaking" because it could lead to an improvement in job performance, which means more money and an increased capacity to afford fun activities.

Focusing on a single skill is the quickest path to instant competence. While you won't achieve "mastery" overnight, you can learn a lot by concentrating on a single outcome for a few weeks or months.

Step 3: Get an education

Sorry to say, but the traditional model of education is slowly dying away. We currently live in a world that's filled with an abundance of information. All you need is Internet access and a desire to learn. Think of it this way—right now, somebody, somewhere has mastered the skill you're trying to learn. Simply find a person who is kind enough to share their experiences and you'll get a world-class education that can't be found in a traditional classroom setting.

Where can you locate expert advice? You can get started by checking out the following websites:

- Amazon.com (read books on the subject).
- Google.com (find information and blogs related to that skill).

- Udemy.com & Skillfeed.com (take an online class on the subject).
- YouTube.com (watch videos that demonstrate a specific concept).
- Facebook.com (connect with authorities who are good at this skill).
- MeetUp.com (join local groups interested in this subject).

Information gathering is the most important part of the process. Your goal here is to get good information and listen to the *right* people. Often, it's better to invest a little money with someone who has a proven track record than to follow a "free" tutorial made by a person who has a limited understanding of the topic.

Cast a wide net and get a variety of information on the subject. Don't just listen to one person's opinion. Instead, do a thorough job with your research. Read a few books/magazines on this topic. Talk to people with a variety of expertise. Do everything you can to fully immerse yourself in this skill.

Step 4: Create a step-by-step plan

This step is also similar to the step-by-step project lists you created for APH #5. Whenever you learn something, immediately apply it. You can do this by taking regular "pauses" in your education and implementing what you've learned. In other words, don't get caught in the trap where you procrastinate on something because you feel like you need more information.

Keep adding items to your skill-based project list and then take action. You'll find that the process of applying information is the fastest way to learn a new skill.

Step 5: Synthesize your notes

At a certain point, you'll have learned and applied a wealth of information. The trick is to turn all of this into a simple-to-follow process. At the point where you feel like you've learned the basics, put everything into a single document. This will help you eliminate redundancy and avoid doing tasks that aren't important.

It's not hard to create an actionable collection of notes. Simply get out your trusty three-ring binder and add a section for the skill you're trying to develop. Be sure to include the following:

- **Reference points**: Annotatebook page numbers, website links, time markings on important audio/video courses and potential tools to use.

- **Step-by-step blueprints**: Same thing—write down a step-by-step process that's recommended by an expert in that skill. Map out any diagrams or flowcharts.

- **Sticking points**: Write down any questions you have about that skill. If possible, ask someone who has proven expert knowledge.

- **Action items**: Figure out a strategy for what you'll do moving forward. Specifically, create a list of habits you can follow on a daily basis that will bring you one step closer to mastery.

Synthesizing information might seem like busywork, but I feel like it's an important part of the process because it helps you *internalize* what you've learned. You'll find that the process of summarizing and eliminating information helps you develop a deeper understanding of the skill.

Step 6: Take daily action

Finally, develop the habit of taking action on a daily basis. Again, you could use <u>Lift.do</u> to track this new routine. Simply find/create a habit that's related to the skill and then track your daily progress.
It's possible to learn almost anything in the world. The challenge is to find the information sources and then develop the habit of taking daily action. For more on how to learn skills in a rapid-fire manner, check out *The First 20 Hours* by Josh Kaufman.

APH #20: Get Secondhand Motivation

Excuse Eliminated: "I don't feel like doing it."

We all have those moments when we're not in the mood to do something. What separates the high achievers from everyone else is that they usually follow through with a task—*even* when they're not feeling up to it. They don't wait for motivation; they have the mindset of being a consistent action taker.

Now, mindset isn't something you can learn overnight. It's a lengthy process that requires repeated exposure to teachings that naturally align with the habits you're trying to develop. Fortunately, there is a simple shortcut to this process. All you have to do is listen to motivational talks/programs throughout the day.

Tapping into inspiring speakers can give you a "shot in the arm" to reinforce and reinvigorate your motivational levels. There are many ways to do this. My two favorite tools are TED Talks and podcasts. Let's go over each.

First there's the TED Talk phenomenon that has grown in popularity over the last few years. TED Talks are a series of speeches from people who are successful in every walk of life. While you can find most of these videos on YouTube, the easiest place to look is the TED.com website.

Furthermore, the TED site breaks down their content into specific categories:

- Being a Student http://www.ted.com/topics/student
- Parenting http://www.ted.com/topics/parenting
- Leadership http://www.ted.com/topics/leadership
- Investment http://www.ted.com/topics/investment
- Health http://www.ted.com/topics/health
- Happiness http://www.ted.com/topics/happiness
- Personal Growth http://www.ted.com/topics/personal+growth
- Success http://www.ted.com/topics/success
- Writing http://www.ted.com/topics/writing
- Visualization http://www.ted.com/topics/visualizations

An alternative to listening to a TED Talk is to subscribe to podcast shows that relate to the specific habit you're trying to develop. Podcasts are easily accessible through the iTunes library, but you can now listen on a variety of mobile devices using Stitcher Radio (http://www.stitcher.com/).

The great thing about this anti-procrastination habit is that you don't use any "free time" in order to do it consistently. It's easy to pop on a speech or podcast while you're at the gym, doing chores or driving. That way you're turning a routine task into an educational environment.

Habit Implementation

This habit requires a small financial investment. In order to access motivational information, you'll need a portable device like an iPod or mobile phone. This can cost a few hundred dollars if you don't already have one.

Here's a simple process for getting started:

1. Get an iPod or mobile phone that uses apps.
2. Download the Stitcher Radio app.
3. Search for shows related to the habit you're trying to develop.
4. Listen to a few different shows and subscribe to your favorites.
5. Watch topic-related videos on the TED website.
6. Get motivated by checking out these programs on a daily basis.

Motivation can wane as a task becomes a daily grind, so a great way to "re-energize" your efforts is to develop the daily habit of listening to inspiring and educational talk shows.

APH #21: Practice Visualization Techniques

Excuse Eliminated: "I don't feel like doing it."

It's easy to become unmotivated when you have a million other things to do. This is true *even* when you have a burning desire to complete a goal. Sure, you might *really* want an outcome, but the process of achieving it often becomes a daily grind. That's why it's important to turn a goal into a living, breathing thing.

Now, I don't really believe in the Law of Attraction, but I do believe there's something to be said for positive thinking and visualizing your goals.

Visualization can work in a variety of ways. You could create a "dream board," where you cut-and-paste goal-related photos into a photo album. You could read empowering books and listen to podcasts. Or you could meditate, imagining what life would be like once you've achieved a goal.

Habit Implementation

I find that visualization works best when it's an occasional habit. You don't necessarily need to do it every day. Instead, it works best when you do it during those moments when you're feeling a significant lack of motivation to follow through with a goal. Here's how that would work:

1. Write a specific, measurable S.M.A.R.T. goal.
2. Create a 5- to 10-minute routine you'll follow when you feel unmotivated.
3. Imagine what it's like to achieve this goal: *How do you feel? Where are you? What is life like? Who is with you?*
4. Repeat this process on a daily basis until you get back those motivational feelings.

I know some people regard visualization as a pseudoscience. However, I think it's a useful routine to follow whenever you're not up to a task. Simply do it whenever you're feeling down, to create energy and excitement for a major goal.

APH #22: Be Patient with the Process

Excuse Eliminated: "It doesn't matter."

We would all like to see instant results. And when they don't happen, it's easy to get frustrated and give up. Often, we lie to ourselves and say a goal doesn't matter, when it actually does.

The important thing to remember is that results don't happen overnight. You need to be patient as you slowly work through a project or goal. There are three ways to do this.

First off, understand that results take time. It's easy to feel like giving up when you don't see an immediate improvement. But usually you won't see instant results with a new routine. Instead, it's an incremental process where you're making small improvements over time.

Next, it's important to celebrate the small wins. When you're building a skill in one particular area, you will achieve breakthroughs. Be sure to reward yourself when they happen (APH #18). Sure, you might not have achieved your long-term goal, but take the time to enjoy a milestone because it will keep you motivated and willing to continue on.

Finally, be ready to hit the occasional plateau. Success isn't always an upward process. Sometimes you'll hit a period where you're not making any forward progress. These are the times when you need to "double down" on your efforts. Identify the 80% activities that bring the best results in your life or business. Then simply do more of them.

Habit Implementation

Some folks have patience and others don't. It's a personality trait that's different from person to person. But if you want to apply *all* of what's taught in this book, then you'll need to develop patience as the ultimate anti-procrastination habit.

Here's a quick way to get started:

1. Ignore any "guru" who promises instant success with a process.
2. Track your progress on a project or habit you're developing.
3. Celebrate and reward yourself when you hit a significant milestone.
4. Avoid beating yourself up when you hit a plateau. Instead, look for ways to "double down" your efforts and build on what's working.

Don't underestimate the importance of patience. Many people give up *right before* they achieve a major breakthrough. Understand that results take time. If you dedicate yourself to a series of daily processes, you'll find yourself slowly inching towards the successful completion of a major goal.

APH #23: Take the 30-Day Challenge

Excuse Eliminated: "I don't have time *right now.*"

Up to this point, we've covered 22 anti-procrastination habits. *The hard part?* There's no possible way you can do them all at once. If you try to implement everything in a single day, you'll become overwhelmed, which ultimately leads to frustration and failure.

Developing great habits is a marathon, not a sprint. It probably took you a number of years to form the routines that cause procrastination, so it would be silly to expect an overnight solution. It's often said that it takes 21 days to start a new habit, but I like the symmetry of doing one each month (or 30 days). In fact, I have a free series called the "30-Day Habit Challenge," (http://www.developgoodhabits.com/30-day-habit-challenge/) where I test a new routine every month. In order to take action on the information contain in this book, I urge you to develop one habit every month.

Habit Implementation

The 30-day challenge works best when you do it on a consistent basis. That's why I recommend you do the following once a month:

1. Identify an anti-procrastination habit that will be most impactful.
2. Map out a day-to-day strategy for how you'll build this habit.
3. Expect setbacks and have a plan for how you'll handle them.
4. At the end of the month, analyze this habit: *Did it work? What did you learn? How can you improve it? Will you keep doing it?*
5. Start a new habit the next month, building on what you've done.
6. Check out the 203 good habits list if you run out of ideas.

I've used the 30-day habit challenge for almost a year now and I can honestly say it's helped me achieve a number of professional and personal breakthroughs. Try it out today by picking the most interesting habit from this book and get started right away.

Conclusion (or "How to Take Action Today")

At the end of every book, I always urge readers to take action. Now this recommendation is more important than ever. You bought this book because you often struggle with procrastination. And the typical response of a procrastinator after reading a book is to say something like, "That was useful information; I'll definitely apply it next week."

Don't do that!

Like you, I've struggled with procrastination. What spurred me into action wasn't reading a book—it was going out and *actually* implementing what I've learned. I urge you to do the same thing.

You've learned 23 ways to fight procrastination. In fact, let's summarize them:

1. Use the 80/20 rule to identify important tasks.
2. Relate every action to a S.M.A.R.T. goal.
3. Capture your ideas whenever they pop up.

4. Create a 43 folders system in your home to process paperwork.
5. Create lists for every multi-step project.
6. Create checklists for routine tasks.
7. Batch similar tasks into single blocks.
8. Single-handle every process and task.
9. Do a review for a few hours each week.
10. Do a monthly review to closely examine your activities.
11. Say "no" to low priority activities.
12. Track your progress and successes.
13. Start your day with the "most important things"(MITs).
14. Prioritize using the ABCDE method.
15. Create a sense of urgency with a time-blocking technique.
16. Become publicly accountable for your goals.
17. Start exceedingly small with a new or routine task.
18. Reward yourself when reaching a milestone.
19. Develop a project-based skill.
20. Get secondhand motivation by listening to inspiring shows.
21. Practice visualization techniques when you feel unmotivated.
22. Be patient with the process of improving your life.
23. Take the 30-Day Challenge to change one habit at a time.

My advice?

Pick one from this list—right now—and get started.

Seriously, I mean it.

As much as I'd love you to review this book and perhaps buy my other titles, I feel the best use of your time is to pick a single habit from the list above and get started right away.

Procrastination doesn't have to control your life. It's entirely possible to become an amazingly productive person. All you have to do is overcome that initial bit of resistance that people get when they learn something new.

It's okay if you fail or slip once in awhile. What's important is to keep at it. Remember, perseverance is one of the true "secrets" to success.

Simply focus on making small improvements every day. Celebrate each victory. And embrace the process of living a productive, exciting life.

Get out there and make things happen!

S.J. Scott
http://www.DevelopGoodHabits.com

Would You Like to Know More?

Overcoming procrastination is an ongoing battle. While you've just learned 23 habits to get things done, it's not always easy to "find time" every day to do them. Fortunately there *is* a simple solution. If you learn how to maximize your sleep schedule, you can wake up each morning energized and ready to work on your *most important tasks*.

In *Wake Up Successful* you'll discover how to build the perfect morning routine that helps you focus on creating energy and finding time to work on your crucial projects.

You can learn more here:
http://www.developgoodhabits.com/book-wakeup

Thank You

Before you go, I'd like to say "thank you" for purchasing my guide.

I know you could have picked from dozens of books on habit development, but you took a chance with my system.

So a big thanks for ordering this book and reading all the way to the end.

Now I'd like ask for a *small* favor. Could you please take a minute or two and leave a review for this book on Amazon?

http://www.developgoodhabits.com/23anti

This feedback will help me continue to write the kind of books that help you get results. And if you loved it, then please let me know :-)

More Books by S.J. Scott

- *Writing Habit Mastery: How to Write 2,000 Words a Day and Forever Cure Writer's Block*

- *Wake Up Successful: How to Increase Your Energy and Achieve Any Goal with a Morning Routine*

- *10,000 Steps Blueprint: The Daily Walking Habit for Healthy Weight Loss and Lifelong Fitness*

- *70 Healthy Habits: How to Eat Better, Feel Great, Get More Energy and Live a Healthy Lifestyle*

About the Author

"Build a Better Life - One Habit at a Time"

Getting more from life doesn't mean following the latest diet craze or motivation program. True success happens when you take action on a daily basis. In other words, it's your habits that help you achieve goals and live the life you've always wanted.

In his books, S.J. provides daily action plans for every area of your life: health, fitness, work and personal relationships. Unlike other personal development guides, his content focuses on taking action. So instead of reading over-hyped strategies that rarely work in the real-world, you'll get information that can be immediately implemented

When not writing, S.J. likes to read, exercise and explore the different parts of the world.

47660953R00070

Made in the USA
Middletown, DE
30 August 2017